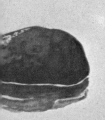

The Knight
in
Crusty Armor

BY VICTORIA COX AND STAN APPLEBAUM
ILLUSTRATED BY GEORGE F. SANDSTRÖM

Under the General Editorship of Vera R. Webster

 GOLDEN PRESS · NEW YORK
WESTERN PUBLISHING COMPANY, INC.
RACINE, WISCONSIN

If I were your size...and you were my size...you might think that I was some sort of robot from outer space.

I walk around on three pairs of legs. My eyes raise and lower on thin stalks, and they turn from side to side as I survey the world around me.

When I find food, I pick it up with a giant claw and bring it to my mouth.

I guess I do look a bit scary in my suit of armor, but I'm not really a monster. I'm not even a fighter, except when I must protect myself. Without my stiff outer coat, I am actually a delicate creature. As a matter of fact, without my stiff outer coating, I would be nothing more than a limp pile of muscles.

I wear my skeleton on the outside with the muscles attached on the inside. That makes me firm enough to stand up and move about quickly. My outside skeleton also protects my soft body from other creatures who find me good to eat.

From the moment I hatch, my life is a
constant struggle for survival. Gulls, herons,
sting rays, serpent stars, squid, octopi, jellyfish,
starfish, and many large fish like to eat me.
I am attacked from the air and from the sea.
Even people catch and eat me.

But, I am more than just a tasty meal. I am a member of Nature's Sanitation Corps. In other words, I am in the cleaning business. Most of my relatives are in the cleaning business also.

As I scurry around on the ocean floor, I often find dead or dying sea creatures as well as decaying plants. These become food for me. If my relatives and I did not eat this material, it would accumulate and pollute the water.

Many creatures living in the sea will not eat food that is not fresh or alive, but I will eat just about anything I can sink my claws into.

I have often thought that I should be knighted for the important job I do. After all, I am performing a great service...helping to keep water areas neat and tidy for all the other creatures who live in the sea. It is even important for those who do not live in the sea.

In a way, I am their "Knight in Crusty Armor." My common, everyday name is Green Crab.

Not all kinds of crabs look like me. But, most crabs have the same basic characteristics—a horizontal segmented body, an exoskeleton, and five pairs of jointed legs.

We usually use our three middle pairs of legs for walking, and our front pair, which have claws at the ends, for grasping and tearing our food. However, our hind legs are either "spiked" or "paddled."

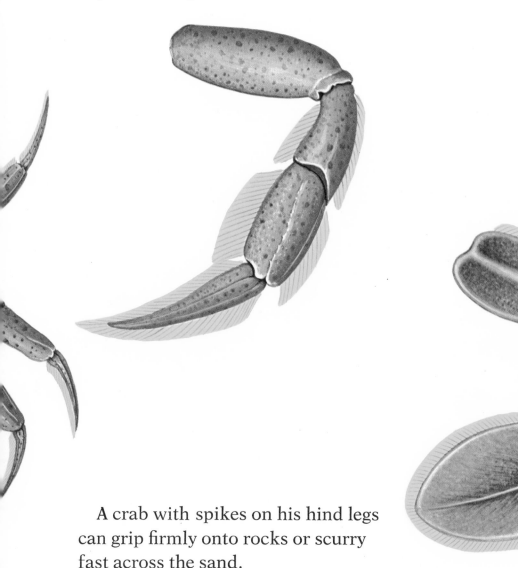

A crab with spikes on his hind legs can grip firmly onto rocks or scurry fast across the sand.

But if a crab has paddles on his hind legs, he can swim.

If you approach one of us while wading in a tide pool, be prepared for a surprise. We will probably scurry away sideways while you are lunging forward. Although some crabs are able to move forward or backwards, walking sideways is our specialty.

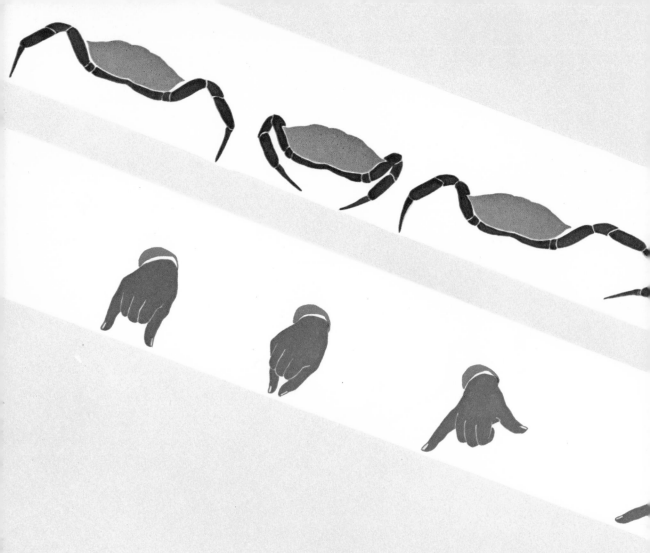

To demonstrate how I move sideways, place
your hand on a flat surface so it looks like a
claw. Lift your middle three fingers and let your
thumb and little finger support your hand. Now,
move your thumb under your palm until it
almost touches your little finger. Then, with the
weight on your thumb, extend your little finger
as far as it will go. With the weight now on your
little finger, lift your thumb and place it under
your palm again. As you repeat this, you can
imitate the way I walk sideways.

If you try moving forward or backwards with your thumb and little finger, you will find that you cannot move as far or as fast.

Since the joints in my legs are hinged, moving sideways is the easiest and fastest way for me to travel.

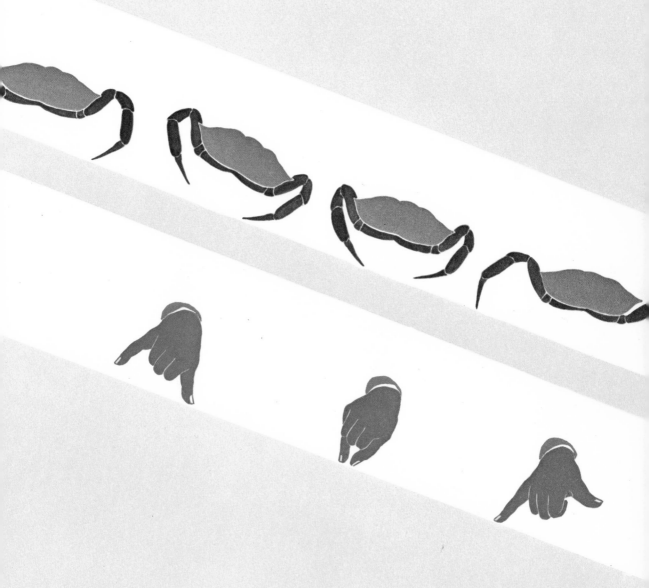

As I move sideways along the ocean floor, tiny paddles under my mouth push fresh sea water through feathery gills. These gills are attached to the upper part of my legs underneath my body. They are my breathing equipment. They absorb oxygen from the water similar to the way your lungs take oxygen from the air.

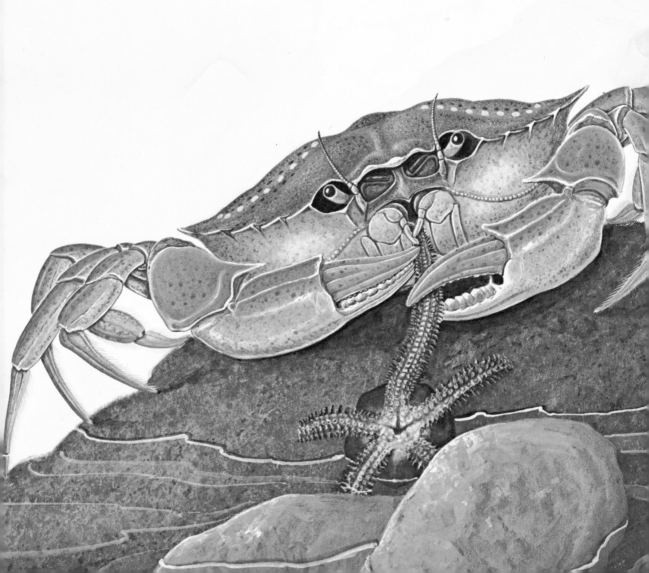

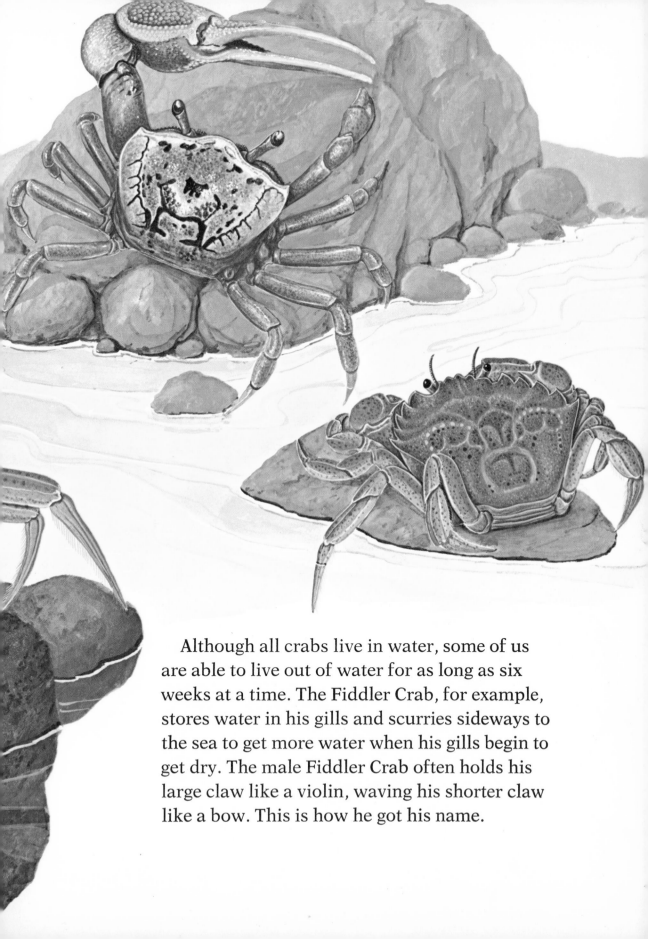

Although all crabs live in water, some of us are able to live out of water for as long as six weeks at a time. The Fiddler Crab, for example, stores water in his gills and scurries sideways to the sea to get more water when his gills begin to get dry. The male Fiddler Crab often holds his large claw like a violin, waving his shorter claw like a bow. This is how he got his name.

I suppose I should tell you about a few of the other characters in my family. Some of them are so odd that you would have to see them to believe them.

Take the Mole Crab, for example. He is only an inch long fully grown and is shaped like a tiny lobster. His legs and claws are tucked under his armor, even when he is moving. But the most unusual thing about this relative is that he does everything backwards. He swims backwards. He crawls backwards. He even digs a hole in the sand backwards.

You can find the Mole Crab on just about any seashore where the waves break. Look for tiny air bubbles oozing from the sand and dig as fast as you can. If you are lucky, you might catch one.

While walking along the beach, if you happen to see a seashell with three pairs of legs sticking out, don't blink your eyes in disbelief. The Hermit Crab, another one of my relatives, is probably living inside.

The Hermit Crab does not have a protective armor on his abdomen, so he moves into an empty seashell for protection. A hook at the end of his body and his last two pairs of legs hold the shell firmly in place.

But the Hermit Crab has a problem. As he grows, he must find a larger shell. While changing shells, the Hermit Crab is without protection, and so he wiggles out of his old shell and jumps backward into a new and larger shell as fast as he can.

In fact, he is probably the world's fastest house changer.

I have another relative in the South Seas that
likes to eat coconuts. He actually climbs
coconut trees and cracks their shells open with
his strong, heavy claws. Although some people
call him the Coconut Crab, more often he is
called the Robber Crab.

Another distant relative is the Horseshoe Crab.
He is shaped like a horse's hoof and has a long
hard tail. He swims upside down, and can only
eat while he is moving. Although he looks fierce,
he is actually harmless to man.

No matter how I differ in appearance from my relatives, we all share one thing in common—a stiff suit of armor, which cannot expand as we grow. There is only one solution. We must shed our armor, grow a bit, and then form a new one. The process is called "molting."

This is how it's done.

When it's time to molt, my body muscles fill with water and expand so much that my armor splits across the rear of my upper shell. At the same time, most of the fluids in my legs and claws flow into my body, shrinking my leg and claw muscles. Finally, as the limy material in my joints dissolves, I am able to slide out of my suit of armor.

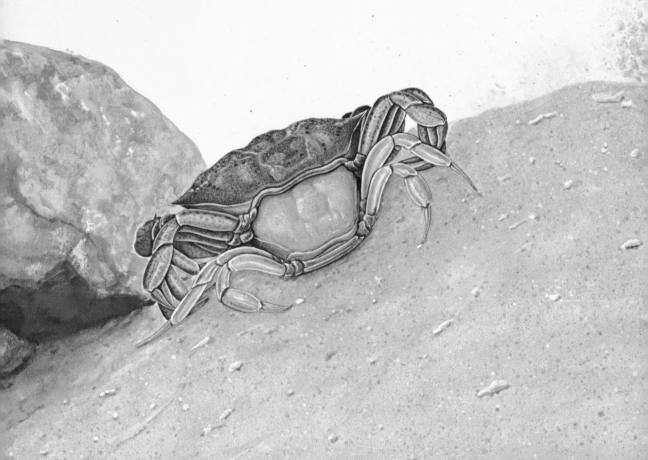

Without my armor, I am without protection. I have to hide for several days while my new coat, which was beginning to form on my body while I was still inside my old one, stretches out and hardens.

Since I do not eat during the molting process, I can't wait to get back to work—eating up all sorts of leftovers on the bottom of the ocean. But, while I am eating, I must keep a constant watch for the other sea creatures that want to make a meal of me.

My tough armor and sharp claws are a ready defense, but sometimes an enemy holds on to my leg or claw while I struggle to get away.

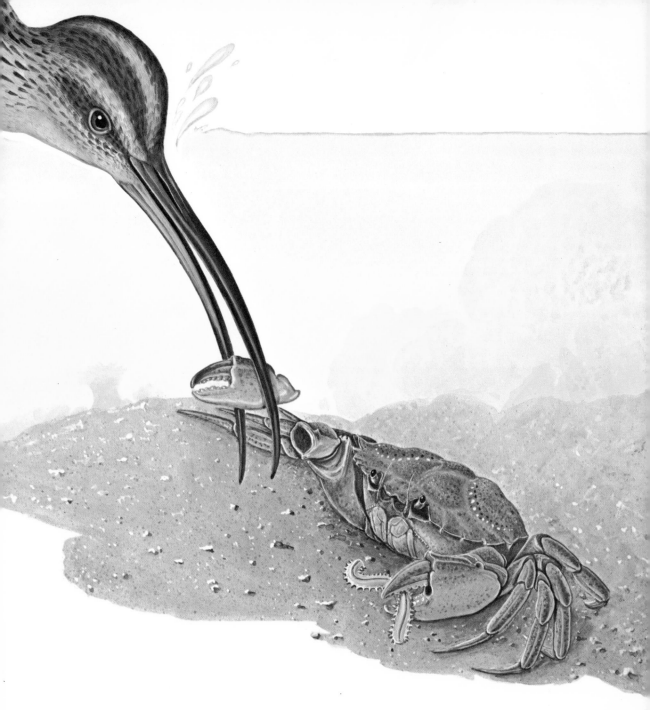

Fortunately, I have a way of escape. I can release a leg or claw at the joint and quickly swim away, when the enemy least expects it. A new leg or claw will grow where the old one used to be.

I have one enemy who is the cleverest of all
and is wise to all my tricks. He often catches me
by tieing a string to a piece of fish and slowly
drawing the bait to the surface of the water. If I
follow the bait, then, quick-as-a-wink, he tries to
scoop me up with his net.

I must keep a sharp look out for this
particular enemy because if I'm not careful...

. . . I could end up in hot water!